SOUTHAMPTON THEN AND NOW

Compiled and photographed
by
ADRIAN RANCE

MILESTONE PUBLICATIONS

Published by Milestone Publications,
62 Murray Road, Horndean, Hampshire PO8 9JL

British Library Cataloguing in Publication Data

Rance, Adrian B.
Southampton : then and now
1. Southampton (Hampshire)—— History
1. Title
942.2'76081 DA690.S7

ISBN 0-903852-78-0

Design Brian Iles

Typeset by Monitor Business Magazine, Hayling Island

Printed and bound in Great Britain by
R.J. Acford, Chichester

Jacket front: Above Bar about 1895
Jacket rear: Above Bar from the Bargate 1945

ACKNOWLEDGEMENTS

The historic photographs in this book are from the collections housed at the Tudor Museum, Southampton.

INTRODUCTION

In recording the process of change over the last one hundred years this book can be enjoyed at two levels. The first is the pleasant enjoyment of nostalgic recollection of how Southampton used to be, recollections that are often all the more pleasant for being seen, as it were, through rose tinted spectacles. On the other level, books such as this show how the city has changed and, in making readers more aware of how the past has shaped the present, will make them anxious to preserve things for the future.

The photographs in the book have been taken for a number of purposes: some are amateur photographs taken perhaps, to record a tram or even a member of the family. Some are official photographs taken to record an event or some municipal enterprise. A large number were taken as commercial photographs for sale as souvenirs in the days when few people had cameras. The selection for this book has been made with a view to illustrating the main types of change that have taken place over the years, starting with the historic centre of the town and moving out to the suburbs.

The main agent of change in Southampton over the last century has been the rapid expansion of the borough. The population of the town in 1841 was some 27,000 people; the population in 1985 is just over 200,000 people. The rapid growth of the mid-Victorian era started with the arrival of the railway from London and the construction of the docks which then attracted the two principal mailship companies, the Royal Mail Line and the P & O. The first spread of housing was eastwards across the open fields of St. Mary's towards the River Itchen. The very nature of Southampton, hemmed in by the River Itchen and the River Test meant that expansion then had to take place in a northward direction. By the 1860's, the town was expanding in two northerly thrusts, separated by the great expanse of Southampton Common in the middle. One thrust was through Freemantle and Shirley on the road towards Romsey and both of these areas became populous suburbs by the middle of the 1860's. The other was through the areas that were to become known as Newtown and Nichols town and thence through Bevois Valley towards Portswood. As the demand for housing land grew, so the parks and estates of the elegant country houses that once surrounded Southampton were sold up for new roads and houses. Now names such as Freemantle, Banisters, Bevois Mount are all that remains of the houses that once attracted the cream of London 'society' to Southampton. Southampton was lucky in that much of this new housing was of good enough quality to survive to the present day and is still good enough to be improved up to modern standards.

By the end of the 19th century, a large portion of the Southampton population was living in areas that were then beyond the boundaries of the borough, which had not been changed since the Middle Ages. The people of Shirley and Freemantle, for instance, had their own local government although they enjoyed most of the advantages of the town, including the tramway system. Despite great opposition from the inhabitants, these areas were incorporated into the borough in 1895. Twelve years earlier an entirely new suburb had been opened up when the National Liberal Land Company built a large number of houses at Bitterne Park and Cobden Bridge to connect it to St. Denys. The next great expansion of the borough came in 1920 when Bassett and Swaythling to the north, and Bitterne, Sholing, Woolston, Weston and Peartree across the River Itchen, were all incorporated into Southampton. Overnight the area of the borough was almost exactly doubled and the Corporation took steps to acquire the Northam toll bridge and the Floating Bridges.

The demand for post-war housing led to the next expansion of the borough and in the 1950's Millbrook and parts of Hound and Netley were incorporated and great new housing estates were developed for the expanding population. The process goes on and the most recent expansion of the borough boundaries was made to accommodate the Lords Hill developments in the 1970's.

The expansion of Southampton into the neighbouring countryside has been matched by the second major factor which has changed the face of the port. This is the gradual reclamation of the mudlands of the lower tidal reaches of the Rivers Test and Itchen. Southampton is on a peninsular hemmed in by water on three sides. Even the name Hamtun or Hamwic means the area 'hemmed' in by water. The view of Southampton across the broad sweep of Western Bay in the River Test was beloved by the romantic painters of the 18th and 19th centuries who depicted Southampton as an idyllic seaside town with the waters reaching up to the stones of the medieval walls. There were no fine beaches however, and even in the Spa Period when sea bathing was at the height of fashion, Southampton's patrons relied on baths filled by the rise and fall of the tide.

The first reclamations from the rivers came with the construction of three quays in the early Middle Ages: the Royal Quay, the West Quay and the Town Quay. From the 17th century to the early 19th century little more was done other than the construction of a small number of private quays on the west bank of the River Itchen. The first major reclamation came with the sale of 216 acres of mudland to the Southampton Dock Company who opened the first dock — now the Princess Alexandra Dock — in 1842. These docks gradually expanded with the construction of an Inner Dock, the Empress Dock and, in the 20th century, the White Star Dock. This book deliberately does not deal with that aspect of the port's development, as it went on beyond the closed-off walls of the dock estate and was beyond the ken of the majority of townsfolk. By contrast, the great reclamations in the River Test affected everybody and fundamentally transformed the nature of Southampton. This reclamation was undertaken by Southern Railway between 1927 and 1933 when a great quay wall was built from near the Royal Pier to Millbrook, enclosing the whole of the great bay in the River Test. In fact reclamation in the River Test had been going on for some time with the construction of the Western Esplanade in the 1850's, the construction of public baths and the building of the electrical power station about 1905. But it was the quay wall of the Western Docks that really changed the scene.

Apart from the two themes of expansion, change has come

about as buildings have been swept away as the needs of the town have changed. Above Bar was transformed from an elegant residential suburb into a busy commercial thoroughfare by the end of the 19th century. The same happened to High Street, the lower part of which contained many public houses and ships' chandlers associated with the maritime life of the town. The pressure of population growth on the older parts of the town also had profound effects. New streets, such as Bernard Street and St. Michael's Street were built to improve access to the congested older parts of the town. Similarly Western Esplanade was built as the result of pressure from the Vicar of St. Michael's. Such was the congestion in the old medieval streets and alleys that major outbreaks of cholera occurred and the 1890's saw the first systematic slum clearance in Southampton. This took place in the Simnel Street area and the first council houses were built. Unfortunately much of the medieval town was swept away, areas which, had they survived, would have matched any medieval streets to be seen in York or Chester.

Between the two world wars Southampton was at the height of its powers. Under the management of Southern Railway, the docks attracted the cream of the passenger liner trade including the great transatlantic liners such as the Queen Mary. The optimistic and confident air of expansion in the borough led to the building of the symbol of its civic pride, the Civic Centre that stands on the high grounds overlooking the reclaimed lands of the Western Docks. The Civic Centre is equal to the great town halls of the Victorian towns of northern England and reflects just that same confidence and big-town status that characterised Liverpool or Manchester. J.B. Priestley visited Southampton in 1933 and recorded that he saw a town that "had not fallen under the evil spell of our times... they are rather proud of themselves down there..."

Soon it was all to change as Southampton took its place in the front line of the war against Hitler. The town was well prepared and had appointed its first Air Raid Controller as early as 1936. The first bombs fell on the town on 20th June 1940 but it was not until a devastating series of blitz raids in November and December of that year that the full extent of aerial warfare became apparent. One double attack on November 30th/December 1st destroyed the historic commercial centre of Southampton. Over 9000 incendiary bombs were dropped together with 800 high explosive bombs. The effect that this had on the life of the citizens was traumatic, and the changes it wrought upon the look of the town were fundamental.

Southampton survived the bombing and went on to play a vital role in the launching of the allied armies in the D-Day invasion of June 1944. The unique role played by Southampton was the amazing cargo handling and shipping operation that sent as much tonnage across to Normandy in four months as the port had handled in the whole of 1938. Plans for the re-building of the town were soon in hand and some grand schemes were committed to paper. In the event the austerity of the post-war years controlled the quality and style of what was built. A large part of the centre of Southampton was taken over for compulsory purchase and comprehensive redevelopment in a uniform style. Unfortunately the style was mediocre and the rebuilt Above Bar and High Street never recovered the magical quality of the pre-war years. Thousands of homes were destroyed by enemy action and post-war priorities were the construction of new houses. Large parts of the city centre were rebuilt and new estates were built at Millbrook, Townhill and Thornhill. As the population, depleted by wartime emergencies, returned to its earlier levels so the expansion of the borough continued again.

Trams came out of service in 1949 thus causing an immediate and noticeable change to the look of many streets but it was the needs of cars that have governed so many changes in recent years. Rural roads that once led to Southampton from places such as Millbrook and Bitterne are now busy dual carriageways, sweeping away many historic features as they were built. A new Northam Bridge and a new Itchen Bridge have been built to speed the motorist on his way; junctions have been widened, roads have been straightened and obstacles swept away. The result is that expanses of tarmac are inevitable features of the modern photographs of this book. One tragedy for the history of Southampton was the construction of the Castle Way inner ring road which cut through the medieval street pattern of Southampton in the 1960's. Conservation is a modern idea and one would hope that such an act of corporate vandalism would not take place today. The result is that the area of the medieval town to be enjoyed by the visitor is much reduced and tucked away behind fast roads.

But cars have not had it all their own way and a great success has been the exclusion of traffic from part of Above Bar and the creation of the pedestrian precinct.

This success will be repeated in the bypassing of Bitterne village and people are now able to shop without the nuisance of cars and lorries. Perhaps one day cars can be excluded from the Town Quay area and Southampton may again enjoy the pleasures of being a seaside town.

This book compares the new with the old. It may help people to appreciate what has gone so that they might strive to ensure that what is good in Southampton now will not be swept away by the developer of the future. This book does not show the best of modern Southampton for that should be the subject of another book.

Adrian Rance
Southampton 1985

CONTENTS

Above Bar from the Bargate — 1945 8
Above Bar from the Bargate — 1985 9
Bargate from Above Bar — 1895 10
Above Bar — 1985 11
Bargate from High Street — 1897 12
Bargate from the High Street — 1985 13
Tudor House Garden — 1927 14
Tudor House Garden — 1985 15
Western Esplanade — 1900 16
Western Esplanade — 1985 17
West Quay — 1890 18
West Quay — 1985 19
The Town Walls at West Quay — 1890 20
The Town Walls — 1985 21
Wickham Court off Vyse Lane — 1895 22
Vyse Lane — 1985 23
French Street — 1910 24
French Street — 1985 25
French Street — 1910 26
French Street — 1985 27
Simnel Street — 1890 28
Simnel Street — 1985 29
Cuckoo Lane — 1920 30
Saxon Gate — 1985 31
Bernard Street — 1910 32
Bernard Street — 1985 33
Oxford Street — 1930 34
Oxford Street — 1985 35
Canal Walk — 1929 36
Canal Walk — 1985 37
Royal Pier — 1910 38
Royal Pier — 1985 39
Town Quay — 1895 40
Town Quay — 1985 41
Town Quay — 1910 42
Town Quay — 1985 43
Porters Lane — 1900 44
Porters Lane — 1985 45
West Street — 1950 46
West Street — 1985 47
High Street — 1897 48
High Street — 1985 49
Above Bar — 1935 50
Above Bar — 1985 51
Above Bar — 1950 52
Guildhall Square — 1985 53
New Road — 1910 54
New Road — 1985 55
Windsor Terrace — 1950 56
Windsor Terrace — 1985 57
The Junction — 1910 58
The Junction — 1985 59
London Road — 1930 60
London Road — 1985 61
The Avenue — 1890 62
The Avenue — 1985 63
The Cowherds — 1910 64
The Cowherds — 1985 65
Southampton Central Station — 1950 66
Southampton Central Station — 1985 67
Millbrook Shore — 1930 68
Millbrook Shore — 1985 69
Gypsy Grove — 1910 70
Gypsy Grove — 1985 71
Shirley High Street — 1905 72
Shirley High Street — 1985 73
Regents Park Road — 1900 74
Regents Park Road — 1985 75
The Cross House — 1906 76
The Cross House — 1985 77
The Floating Bridge — 1945 78
The Floating Bridge Hard — 1985 79
Victoria Road, Woolston — 1904 80
Victoria Road, Woolston — 1985 81
Weston Lane — 1910 82
Weston Lane — 1985 83
Lances Hill — 1910 84
Lances Hill — 1985 85
Northam Bridge Road — 1910 86
Northam Bridge Road — 1985 87
Highfield Church — 1905 88
Highfield Crescent — 1985 89
Mayfield Road — 1912 90
Mayfield Road — 1985 91
Swaythling — 1905 92
Swaythling — 1985 93
Millbrook — 1920 94
Millbrook — 1985 95

ABOVE BAR FROM THE BARGATE — 1945 *This photograph was taken after the rubble and chaos caused by the bombs of the blitz had been cleared away. During the nights of November 30th and December 1st 1940, 800 high explosive bombs were followed by 9000 incendiary bombs which caused uncontrollable fires.*

ABOVE BAR FROM THE BARGATE — 1985 *The individual plots of land, still to be seen in the lines of bomb scarred walls in the previous photograph, were swept away by comprehensive redevelopment. The architectural style of the new buildings reflect the economic austerity of the post-war years and has been described as 'watered-down neo-Georgian'.*

BARGATE FROM ABOVE BAR — 1895 *Taken before the horse trams were electrified in 1899, this picture shows how the suburban houses of the 19th century have been taken over as shops. The man on the left is standing by the gateway to the Above Bar Congregational Church, famous for its associations with the hymn writer, Isaac Watts.*

ABOVE BAR — 1985 *Marks and Spencer is now on the site of the Above Bar Congregational Church. One of the better post-war achievements has been the introduction of a pedestrian precinct in a large part of Above Bar. Here shoppers can stroll, free from the nuisance of traffic. The Bargate still dominates the distant view of course.*

BARGATE FROM HIGH STREET — 1897 *Horse drawn traffic, including the trams, dominate High Street and all of it had to pass through the central arch of the Bargate. All Saints Church with its impressive Ionic colonnade was built at the corner of High Street and East Street in the 1790's and it survived until the bombing of 1940.*

BARGATE FROM THE HIGH STREET — 1985 *The roads around the Bargate were built in the 1930's when the medieval monument ceased to be an obstacle to traffic and became stranded on its own traffic island. The result is that the modern High Street has lost the closed-in comfortable look and the modern flat skyline does little to add interest to the view.*

TUDOR HOUSE GARDEN — 1927 *Perhaps the most fundamental change to the face of Southampton has been the reclamation of land from the River Test between 1927 and 1933 when Southern Railway built the Western Docks. This view from Tudor House Garden shows the quay wall of the docks extension under construction.*

TUDOR HOUSE GARDEN — 1985 *The distant view over the town wall is now dominated by the Western Docks and the Post House Hotel, built as the Skyway Hotel in the mid 1960's. The garden itself has been redesigned into an authentic Elizabethan Garden instead of what was thought to be a Tudor Garden when the museum was opened in 1912.*

WESTERN ESPLANADE — 1900 *The waters of the River Test came right up to the town walls when they were built in the 14th century. Western Esplanade was built in the 1850's largely as a result of pressure from the Vicar of St. Michael's who wanted a new road to improve access into his parish. Forest View at the top of the walls was built about the same time.*

WESTERN ESPLANADE — 1985 *The buildings of West Quay have been cleared and the view opened up to the West Gate in the distance. During the week the road is full of speeding cars and motorists are lucky to find an empty parking meter. The trees on the right conceal the Pirelli factory built on the reclaimed land of the River Test.*

WEST QUAY — 1890 *When the photograph was taken the only land reclamation was around the medieval West Quay. From the Royal Pier one could see right across the bay to the houses of Blechynden and Four Posts. On the right is the Harbour Board yard that was cleared when Western Esplanade was extended to link West Quay and Royal Pier in the 1890's.*

WEST QUAY — 1985 *The previous photograph was taken from the site of what is now Mayflower Park. This, slightly different perspective, shows how the town wall has been exposed to view and how roads, roundabouts and the Central Baths occupy the moorings of earlier fishing boats and dinghies. The process of reclamation has been gradual, and in the First World War a railway was built here.*

THE TOWN WALLS AT WEST QUAY — 1890 *The walls were a favourite playground of the children in the older part of town. Haddon and Beavis the coal merchants had stables in the 12th century Norman House, the roof of which can be seen over the walls. On the left is the Long Rooms, famous as the Assemblies Room in the time when Southampton was a spa town.*

THE TOWN WALLS — 1985 *Western Esplanade is much wider and the distant view is now dominated by Arundel Towers, a pair of office blocks built on the site of the original Spa Garden. The doorway into the Norman House has been blocked up with stone that is now carefully protected by law as a medieval monument although it is only 80 years old.*

WICKHAM COURT OFF VYSE LANE — 1895 *St. Michael's Parish was full of small courts and alleyways nesting between the medieval streets of the town. Vyse Lane was one of the original medieval lanes and ran between Bugle Street and French Street. This area contained many slums until they were cleared in the 1890's.*

VYSE LANE — 1985 *The Duke of Wellington is still on the right although it is now a black-and-white building rather than the weather boarded building of the last photograph. The view across Bugle Street to the Westgate is now opened up and post-war flats occupy the site of Wickham Court. The line of Vyse Lane is preserved in the line of the pavement.*

FRENCH STREET — 1910 *Running north from Town Quay, French Street was one of the original streets of the medieval town, named after the French immigrants settled at the time of the Norman Conquest. During the Spa period the town's theatre was in French Street, and, with the lamp posts outside, the Empire Palace continued the tradition on the same site.*

FRENCH STREET — 1985 *The warehouse, built at the turn of this century and called Eagle Warehouse, is now the City's archaeological research centre. In the distance the old Bull Inn, which survived the war, has been found to be the most complete 13th century merchants house in the country and is now being restored.*

FRENCH STREET — 1910 *Looking south the eagle of Eagle Warehouse can.be seen in the distance as can the old Bull Inn. On the left is the rear of the Audit House, giving access to the Fish Market whilst further down on the left is 41, French Street, the home of Southampton's famous son, Isaac Watts and the site of Southampton's post office in the early 19th century.*

FRENCH STREET — 1985 *Much of the area was destroyed by bombing and Phippards, the wall paper manufacturers have been replaced by post-war Corporation housing. The line of French Street was destroyed in the 1960's by the construction of Castle Way, but the long tradition of markets in the area survives to the present day.*

SIMNEL STREET — 1890 *This photograph shows the medieval street which led down to Biddlesgate near West Quay. Many of the houses are probably medieval but much of this area was cleared in the mid 1890's as part of the Simnel Street Improvement Plan, the first slum clearance scheme in Southampton. The first council houses were built as part of this scheme.*

SIMNEL STREET — 1985 *Once again the area has been comprehensively redeveloped, this time with flats and houses belonging to a housing corporation. Simnel Street is now a pedestrian walkway and new life has come to this part of Southampton. Two houses of the 1890's scheme can be seen in the background, deliberately preserved as part of the history of the area.*

CUCKOO LANE — 1920 *The area between Bugle Street and Cuckoo Lane which ran south from the Westgate inside the town walls, was packed with 18th and 19th century housing. The Westgate itself was leased by the Corporation as a cottage and the weather-boarded "Old Guard House" was largely unused and belonged to a house known as Madame Maes' house.*

SAXON GATE — 1985 *The houses were demolished some years ago and the area stood as an open 'green'. Now townhouses and new landscaping provide a pleasant setting for the Westgate and the Old Guard House, re-named Tudor Merchants Hall. In fact it is neither Tudor nor a merchant's house: it has been shown to be a 15th century market hall moved to the site in the 17th century.*

BERNARD STREET — 1910 *The clock on Holy Rood Church proclaims this photograph to have been taken at 12.30 in the afternoon. It may be that the group of men are waiting for casual work either in the markets or in the nearby docks. Certainly there are more people around that one would find in Bernard Street today.*

BERNARD STREET — 1985 *Holy Rood lost its spire in the bombing and the ruins of the church are laid out as a memorial to the men and women of the Merchant Navy who gave their lives in that war. Very few of the pre-war buildings survive and the scene is now dominated by St. Cross House, the elegant headquarters of the DHSS where those in need of work today receive their benefits.*

OXFORD STREET — 1930 *This part of Southampton was developed in the mid-19th century following the arrival of the railway and the development of the docks. This was a prosperous business area by the end of the 19th century — much of it connected with the docks. The Royal Mail building is on the left while Rayners, suppliers of uniforms to the Merchant Navy, is on the right.*

OXFORD STREET — 1985 *Many of the Victorian buildings survive and the street is in a designated conservation area. The street is now blocked at its junction with Terminus Terrace and the traction poles are the only relics of the trams that used to come down here. The Sailors' Home in the distance is now a Salvation Army Hostel.*

CANAL WALK — 1929 *The street runs along the line of the medieval ditches that ran outside the eastern defences of the walled town. The name recalls the fact that the ditches were used to carry a branch of the Southampton to Salisbury Canal which was started in 1795 and which went bankrupt immediately after its completion a few years later.*

CANAL WALK — 1985 *The area was extensively damaged in the wartime blitz and the shops have never returned. A multi-storey car park serves the needs of those shopping elsewhere and industrial buildings have gone up on the other side of the street. The community spirit of the 1930's no longer exists here.*

ROYAL PIER — 1910 *The pier was first opened in 1833 and was enlarged and rebuilt in 1891. The paddle steamers of both Red Funnel and Campbell's were familiar sights here until 1939. In this picture the PS Princess Helena, built in 1895, is at one of the berths. The railway line and the station on the Royal Pier lasted until about 1913.*

ROYAL PIER — 1985 *The 1891 entrance piers are there today but in a slightly different position. The familiar domed entrance building was built in the late 1920's when a new railway was constructed to link the old docks with the new Western Docks. The railway is now gone, the pier is derelict and the view to the old ballroom is obscured by modern buildings.*

TOWN QUAY — 1895 *The Town Quay was the principal quay of the town from the 15th century until the construction of the docks in the 1830's. When this photograph was taken the quay can be seen crowded with sailing ships, schooners, ketches, barges and the like, all of which carried the bulk of coastal traffic in the 19th century.*

TOWN QUAY — 1985 *Many changes have taken place: the water in front of the roadway was reclaimed in the 1920's, more buildings have been constructed on the quay itself and the Harbour Board Offices were opened in 1925. Modern shipping is there in the form of the Red Funnel Ferries to the Isle of Wight and a marina is proposed for much of the area.*

TOWN QUAY — 1910 *Great brick warehouses, public houses, common lodging houses and houses of ill repute were characteristic of the Edwardian Town Quay area. This warehouse stood at the bottom of French Street; it was a grain warehouse and sacks can be seen in the hoist doorways. A & F Ray were large corn factors who owned Woodmill on the River Itchen at this time.*

TOWN QUAY — 1985 *Despite long standing plans to demolish it, Geddes Warehouse, formerly known as 'H' Baggage Warehouse, has survived to become an important part of the maritime heritage. The corner can be seen in the photograph and it is now being converted into modern luxury flats. Garages are being built in a style thought to imitate the Victorian warehouse.*

PORTERS LANE — 1900 *Running behind the warehouses of the Town Quay, Porters Lane contained a number of common lodging houses used by sailors and dock workers. The fine 12th century house known as Canute's Palace, was occupied by Haddon and Beavis, the coal merchants and the gable wall of the Anchor and Hope suggests that this too was a medieval house.*

PORTERS LANE — 1985 *Canute's Palace and the surrounding area is still much as it was left after the wartime bombing. Geddes Warehouse, on the south of the lane, and the warehouse on High Street, are the only reminders of the Victorian commercial development. When the area is eventually redeveloped an opportunity will exist for the presentation of a fine group of medieval monuments.*

WEST STREET — 1950 *One of the medieval streets, West Street, linked High Street with Simnel Street and thence to West Quay. Following the wartime destruction, this view was opened up to St Michael's Church and when the photograph was taken, a temporary Nissen hut remained on the cleared ground.*

WEST STREET — 1985 *The post-war development may not have much to recommend it in architectural terms, but at least the tradition of public houses in the area has been retained. On the right is the Southerner, while the Queens occupies the far corner of West Street. The cellar of the earlier medieval house is still preserved under the Queens.*

HIGH STREET — 1897 *Delivery boys, tradesmens' carts, ice being delivered on a flat bed cart, a horse tram in the distance, ladies out shopping and the boy with the perambulator: all this a glimpse of life in Southampton towards the end of the Victorian era. The numerous black flags on the buildings may denote some national day of mourning.*

HIGH STREET — 1985 *Still a wide spacious High Street but one cannot linger on the roadway today. Some of the Victorian commercial buildings survive as does the Dolphin Hotel, but the drabness of the post-war buildings, with their flat skylines, emphasises the sad loss of so many fine buildings over the years. St. Lawrence's Church was pulled down 1925.*

ABOVE BAR — 1935 *This is Above Bar as J.B. Priestley would have seen it when he visited and wrote about Southampton. In the distance the Gas Company is in the old Royal Hotel building and, on the corner of Pound Tree Road is Alfred Priddis, milliner. The Street was full of small shops such as George Gillet, the butchers shop.*

ABOVE BAR — 1985 *The junction of Above Bar with Pound Tree Road has been widened and is a major thoroughfare. Modern buses now use this part of Above Bar with the frequency that the trams did fifty years ago. The pedestrian precinct has cut off the lower part of the street to traffic and Woolworth's is on the site of the Gas Company offices.*

ABOVE BAR — 1950 *The bombing of Above Bar during the blitz in November and December 1940, spawned a crop of single storey emergency buildings as temporary accommodation for the destroyed shops. The shortage of building licences delayed the reconstruction of Above Bar until the mid-1950's but now only one wartime building survives. This is the Sun Inn at the bottom of High Street.*

GUILDHALL SQUARE — 1985 *Described by Pevsner as "the only piece of imaginative post-war planning in the whole of the Above Bar area", Guildhall Square opens up a view of the Guildhall from Above Bar where the temporary shops stood. Even this, however, is a temporary scheme awaiting the implementation of the original proposals made in the 1960's.*

NEW ROAD — 1910 *A prominent feature of the junction between Above Bar and New Road was the clock tower built in 1889 and presented to the town by Mrs Henrietta Bellenden Sayers. Tram No. 11 was one of the first electric tramcars purchased by the Corporation when it took over the tramways in 1899.*

NEW ROAD — 1985 *The Clock Tower was moved to Bitterne Triangle in 1935 when the Civic Centre Road was built and the junction with New Road improved. This provided an important new east-west route through Southampton and the tower was moved as a hazard to traffic. Palmerston Park is much the same but the Atlantean buses provide a more comfortable form of public transport.*

WINDSOR TERRACE — 1950 *This small street runs behind the houses on Above Bar near Civic Centre Road and is named after the Windsor Hotel, now a public house. On the left is the canopy of the Grand Theatre which was opened in 1898 and which had a long tradition of theatrical entertainment until its closure in 1960.*

WINDSOR TERRACE — 1985 *The Grand Theatre and all the houses in the earlier photograph were demolished in 1960 and a comprehensive re-development of the area took place. Marlands House was built on the site of the theatre and new shops, including Plested's pie shop, were built. A new bus station was built on the site of Birmingham Street immediately to the west.*

THE JUNCTION — 1910 *This was the junction between the Shirley and the Portswood branches of the tramway system. Here a 'pointsboy' operated the points until they were automated in 1914. The Plummer Roddis store occupies the corner of Above Bar and Commercial Road; this was founded in 1898 as Plummer, Roddis and Tyrell Ltd.*

THE JUNCTION — 1985 *Plummers was destroyed by the German Air Force in 1940 and, after many years in temporary buildings, the store was rebuilt in the 1960's. It is now part of the Debenhams Group. Modern bus passengers still ask for the 'Junction' although few realise the significance of the name.*

LONDON ROAD — 1930 *The motor car is beginning to make its mark on Southampton. A census taken in 1929 recorded over 3000 cars and 6000 bicycles using London Road in one April day. A distinctive feature of this photograph is the tram with its covered top deck designed particularly to fit under the Bargate arch.*

LONDON ROAD — 1985 *Although the post-war rebuilding has altered the character of the buildings, much is still the same as it was 50 years ago. One loss to the skyline is the Unitarian Church of St. Paul's, designed by Philip Brannon and opened in 1860 but many of the estate agents have their offices here much as they did in the 1930's.*

THE AVENUE — 1890 *The Avenue was laid out as a turnpike road across Southampton Common in the 18th Century. Since then it has retained its reputation as one of the finest approaches into a city anywhere in southern England. The horse tramlines and the houses are signs of the gradual expansion of Southampton towards the Common in the 19th century.*

THE AVENUE — 1985 *Many of the trees are gone but others have been planted. The houses at the junction of Avenue Road are still there but the trams have long since gone. On a Sunday morning one can still enjoy a stroll along the Avenue but during the week, cars and lorries make it quite unpleasant for pedestrians.*

THE COWHERDS — 1910 *Once the residence of the official appointed by the town to look after the Common and the cattle grazing on it — hence the name. The Cowherds has been an inn for many years but at the turn of the century the needs of the traveller were very different: hence the advertisement for livery stables.*

THE COWHERDS — 1985 *The hooped sign is still there and flagpoles still decorate the outside of the pub. There have been some additions to the building but it is much the same as it was eighty years ago. Although the motor car dominates the scene, The Cowherds is still a favourite with citizens enjoying a stroll on the Common.*

SOUTHAMPTON CENTRAL STATION — 1950 *When the Clock Tower was built in 1895 the station was known as Southampton West; it was renamed Central in July 1935 and the tower remained a landmark of the area. This photograph shows the scars of war which are to be seen with the Nissen hut and the single storey war-time emergency pub on the site of its bombed predecessor.*

SOUTHAMPTON CENTRAL STATION — 1985 *The whole area has been the subject of a comprehensive redevelopment: Overline House on the left was built on the site of the 1895 station buildings when the line was electrified in 1967. The office blocks known as Nelson Gate were completed in the late 1970's.*

MILLBROOK SHORE — 1930 *A pleasant promenade ran along the railway line overlooked by the houses of Four Posts. This was a popular spot for sunbathers and swimmers until this part of the river was reclaimed during the construction of the Western Docks. To compensate for this loss of foreshore a new park was laid out and was named Mayflower Park.*

MILLBROOK SHORE — 1985 *The trees of Elmfield are still a feature of the distant view but the scene has been changed by the construction of a road bridge across the railway in the 1930's. This photograph is taken from the bridge and shows how the station has expanded westwards, how the houses of Four Posts have been replaced by industrial buildings and how Mountbatten Way runs where the waters of the Test used to flow.*

GYPSY GROVE — 1910 *This secluded lane runs from Shirley Road across open land towards St. James Road. It was the southern boundary of the Whitedwood Park estate which was bounded by Shirley Road on the west, St. James Road on the east and Howards Grove on the north.*

GYPSY GROVE — 1985 *The development of the area started with the Whitedwood Estate Company formed in 1908 and some of the area near Gypsy Grove was developed in a garden city tradition before the First World War. Now the whole area is built up and Gypsy Grove is bounded on each side by garden walls.*

SHIRLEY HIGH STREET — 1905 *Shirley was not incorporated into the Borough until the 1890's and the newly electrified Shirley tramline was inaugurated on 22nd January 1900. Car No. 17 is seen heading towards the town Junction and pedestrians seem to outnumber the vehicles on the road.*

SHIRLEY HIGH STREET — 1985 *Many of the buildings are the same but the junction with Park Street is now controlled by lights. The trams previously turned into Park Street to reach the Shirley depot which has served horse trams, electric trams and motor buses. It is now empty and awaiting redevelopment, probably for shops.*

REGENTS PARK ROAD — 1900 *Regents Park was laid out as a spacious and quiet suburb of elegant 'villas' in the mid 19th century. The approach to the estate from Shirley was guarded by carriage gates and a small gate-keeper's lodge. On a sunny day it was evidently a pleasant place for the children to play.*

REGENTS PARK ROAD — 1985 *The gateway has gone but the lodge remains at the junction of Edmund Road and Regents Park Road. The area is still a quiet residential suburb although few of the original villas survive. The Thorner Charity buildings were relocated here when the original institution in Above Bar was demolished for the construction of Civic Centre Road in the 1930's.*

THE CROSS HOUSE — 1906 *The Cross House shelter dates at least from the 17th century and probably incorporates a medieval boundary cross of the borough. The shelter was built for the convenience of travellers waiting for a rowing ferry boat across the River Itchen and was clearly a favourite playground for local children.*

THE CROSS HOUSE — 1985 *The structure is looking sad without its roof but plans are now in hand for rebuilding it. Many of the industrial buildings are now gone but the sheds of the Corporation depot can still be seen. Some attempt is being made to improve the area with landscaping and to improve public access to the waterfront but there are few children to play here now.*

THE FLOATING BRIDGE — 1945 *Near to the Cross House the floating bridge operated across the River Itchen, connecting the Cross House with Woolston. The bridge was opened in 1836 and is photographed here in February 1945, showing the Hotchkiss machine gun manned by HMS Safeguard. The bombed Supermarine Works are in the background.*

THE FLOATING BRIDGE HARD — 1985 *The Floating Bridge service came to an end on June 11th 1977, ten days after the soaring white and elegant Itchen Bridge was opened to the public. Now little survives to remind the passer-by of the floating bridge tradition and the hard is closed off behind barbed wire.*

VICTORIA ROAD, WOOLSTON — 1904 *Woolston grew as a result of the shipyard established there in 1876 by T.R. Oswald, later Oswald Morduant. The yard built a large number of iron three-masted sailing ships for use all over the world. At the end of the 19th century there was a plan to build a dry dock here and for Woolston to become Southampton's 'Birkenhead'.*

VICTORIA ROAD, WOOLSTON — 1985 *On the face of it little has changed. The shipyard is now Vosper Thornycroft and many of the earlier buildings survive. Before the construction of the Itchen Bridge which can be seen in the distance, the Floating Bridge connected Woolston with the Southampton shore. Now bus services are greatly enhanced and the No. 9 runs to Shirley.*

WESTON LANE — 1910 *Weston Grove House was built about 1802 and the estate reached up both sides of Weston Lane as far as Wright's Hill. Two arches were constructed to take a carriageway across the lane thus completing a circuit of the estate. One of the bridges was demolished in 1931 and the other as late as 1948.*

WESTON LANE — 1985 *The careful observer might notice the earthen banks that carried the carriageway up to the vanished arches. The Sun Inn is still there but the Weston Grove estate and the later Mayfield House estate have been extensively developed for housing since 1945.*

LANCES HILL — 1910 *This part of the Portsmouth Road linking Bitterne Manor with Bitterne village is named after the Lance family who owned Chessel House at the beginning of the 19th century. The toll gate was near the top of the hill and the road was freed from tolls in March 1929 when the Corporation purchased the Northam Bridge Company.*

LANCES HILL — 1985 *The trees have matured and the house is still there at the junction of Juniper Road. The traffic now speeds past on a fast dual carriageway and pedestrians can no longer wander on the road. The houses on the left were built when the Chessel House estate was developed in the 1930's.*

NORTHAM BRIDGE ROAD — 1910 *The main road to Portsmouth running up to Bitterne from the Northam Bridge runs through the estates of Bitterne Manor. By the turn of the present century these houses had gone up on the site of the Roman town of Clausentum and the road was quiet and rural.*

NORTHAM BRIDGE ROAD — 1985 *The area to the east of the River Itchen was incorporated into the Borough of Southampton in 1920. The houses are still there but the road is a major approach road into the city centre. Four lanes wide, it has taken much of the front gardens and crash barriers are reminders that this is an accident black spot.*

HIGHFIELD CHURCH — 1905 *Highfield Church was built to serve the expanding population of this northerly suburb of Southampton in 1846. The east end was reconstructed in 1878 to form the larger chancel to be seen in this picture. The setting was delightfully rural and children, perhaps from the Sunday School, are walking across the old gravel workings.*

HIGHFIELD CRESCENT — 1985 *The footpath in the previous photograph survives and runs up between the houses in Highfield Crescent thus allowing a glimpse of the church across the valley. Housing has covered all of the area between Welbeck Avenue and Highfield Lane and, being close to the University, is now much sought after.*

MAYFIELD ROAD — 1912 *Miss E.H. Cox owned this shop at the corner of Mayfield Road and Woodcote Road between 1912 and 1914. The area was developed for housing as the Hampton Park estate in the 1890's and, looking over the River Itchen, it grew to be an extensive suburb. Prior to the extension of the tramways from Portswood, the area was served by horse buses.*

MAYFIELD ROAD — 1985 *The corner shop is still there but the name is different. A plastic lean-to has been added to protect the display of fruit and vegetables. As is often the case, the corner shops of Southampton have been saved from extinction by the enterprise of Asian newcomers to the City.*

SWAYTHLING — 1905 *This part of Southampton was essentially rural with farms and the Corporation waterworks as the main features. Its importance as a suburb, however, is underlined by the decision to build a railway station here. This view looks down Wessex Lane to the Baker's Arms opposite the station.*

SWAYTHLING — 1985 *Modern housing has replaced the thatched cottages on the right but otherwise the view is much as before. Modern traffic and the nuisance of the A27 make this an unpleasant place in which to linger now and the area has for some time been under the blight of a threatened link to the new M27.*

MILLBROOK — 1920 *A small village to the west of Southampton on the main road to Bournemouth and Salisbury. The view is looking towards Redbridge with Wimpsom Lane on the right. In the foreground is Millbrook Pond and the road on the left goes down to Pondside Farm which survived until recent years.*

MILLBROOK — 1985 *The same view, looking across Millbrook Road to the Fighting Cocks shows how the old village is now totally gone. The site is occupied by a large roundabout and flyover. The approaches into Southampton from the west have been gradually improved over the years and now comprises dual carriageway from Totton right through to the city centre.*

Milestone Publications, publishers of the highly successful 'Down Memory Lane' nostalgic local history series, invite you to view their current issues at all South Hampshire booksellers and many newsagents, or wrote for a complete list to:

Milestone Publications
62 Murray Road,
Horndean,
Hampshire